Anamika Praveen

Myself, Anamika Praveen.
I'm an 11th-grade student at Sharjah Indian School in the United Arab Emirates.
My hobbies include reading, writing, drawing, photography, and dancing. My first book, Sorrow and Glee(poem) was published in the year 2023.

Father   : Praveen Radhakrishnan
Mother : Soumya Praveen
Sister   : Malavika Praveen

English Language
26th July 2016
(Novel)
by
Anamika Praveen

♦

Published in November 2024
by Kairali Books Private Limited
Thalikkavu Road, Kannur.
Ph : 0497-2761200
E-Mail : kairalibooksknr@gmail.com

♦

Illustrations
Anamika Praveen

♦

Cover Design
Soumya Praveen

♦

75/24-25/Sl.No.1642/200/NS.18.6
ISBN 978-93-5973-419-4

26th July 2016

Anamika Praveen

Kairali Books

To my mom,
Thank you for being
my best friend and my strength.

A teeming teenage novel
Jacob Abraham

Teenage is beautiful but stressful. It is a juncture between childhood and adulthood. Sometimes we don't know where the boundaries blur and become visible. In literature, teenage love was always featured with much celebration. From Jane Austen to Harper Lee, many authors had penned their best in this category. It's not a simple job to write a novel based on teenage-hood.

Here, Anamika is coming up with a wonderful teenage novel about love and longing, betrayal and forgetting. I am sure she strode on a confident path in writing this small novel based on her own convictions as a teenager. This teenage novelist explores her characters with a vivid reflection of life. They tread on the threshold of new territories.

While reading this novel, I went back to my teenage days down the memory lane and conjured many sweet memories. When you start reading this book, your heart will also pulsate with a newness.

As a writer, I appreciate this young writer for her use of certain tools to tell the story. One is diary notes and the other letters. To glue her reader in the text, she has used these narrative techniques wisely.

I am not telling anything about the plot in this simple preface. You have to explore it your own way. One thing too certain to me is that this young writer has a long way to go with her mighty pen. She has all attributes to explore life with the eyes of a writer. Great literary journey ahead, dear Anamika.

Author's Note

"His love was forbidden but he risked his life for it because without it he had no life"

-

Valorem

Words in the dictionary aren't enough to define LOVE.

This is not much of an author's note, but all I want to say is that different people have different images of love and my image of love is expressed through this book. And with all my heart, I believe that this kind of love does exist.

Love is not always worth the pain it causes. However, the time in your life when you are in love is truly wonderful.

No matter how hard some things hurt you, you have to accept it. It's difficult to let go of things, but what if there's no other option?

Foreword

I would like to thank everyone who helped me in finishing this novel. I keep the gratitude in my heart to my mom and dad for supporting me and being my back bone, my sister who has been patiently waiting for the novel since the beginning of writing and Anuja aunty for reading this novel and giving me a very valuable feedback.

CONTENTS

Characters

Nitara
Abhiram (Abhi)
Ekantika (Eka)
Ninad

Those Few Words

I had this urge
to tell you a few words.
I wanted to tell you that,
every time we met.
As you talked about your day,
My words lay on the tip of my tongue,
battling to come out.
The way your eyes sparkled,
the life in you shined,
the happiness you radiated,
all meant a lot to me.
I could not hold on to those words.
I had no energy to battle with those words.
but I still hold those words with me.
And I finally said it
when you started to walk away.
I whispered those words,
"I LOVE YOU"
As you walked away,
but you never heard those words…

Chapter 1

Pain

"I am sorry, but she is in a coma." her condition is very critical. Her head got hit to something very hard."

His eyes widened and got filled with tears. It seems as if he was trying to hold those tears, but they spilled over down to his cheeks. He was not able to process what the doctor just said.

"Abhi!" the doctor called.

"You can go see her." The doctor offered gently.

He walked towards the ICU, his mind clouded with so many thoughts. "Will she be able to recognize me?" he muttered under his breath.

He opened the door. There she was, lying in the bed, still and fragile with oxygen masks on. Her eyes were closed.

"Will she remember me?" he muttered again.

He went and stood near her, tears flowing down

through his cheeks, he held her hand and said,

"I am here for you!"

Tears kept streaming down his cheeks uncontrollably. He wondered, "Where will all these tears end up?"

He stood there staring at her closed eyes. The mutual thing they both shared at that moment was pain. PAIN…. The pain that he was suffering was clearly seen in his eyes but her pain was within and was not openly evident in her dormant body except those eyes…They remained closed the whole time.

He felt like time stretching out painfully, each moment dragging on as if it were never-ending. He wished for the world to shatter into fragments, hoping that those pieces would never come back again. He wanted to scream aloud, but his voice was not coming out as if the words were stuck in his throat. It was raining outside. The sky and the entire universe seemed to be crying for him.

"If I was there at home, this wouldn't have happened. He thought. It was haunting him. He felt like it was his mistake leaving her home alone. He left the room, but his soul felt anchored there, near her, with her.

Her name lingered in his heart, Nitara....

Chapter 2

HER

Her eyes were doe-like eyes. Beautiful. When silence hit her, it was her eyes that spoke. He was indeed addicted to her. She was his courage, his strength, his life, his soul and everything.

It was love at first sight. He saw her for the first time in his office. He used to watch her daily. Over time, they grew closer and became friends. And one day he proposed to her and she said YES. Then they got married, beginning a new chapter together.

He craved to see her smile. He would do anything to make her smile. She was a part of him. In fact, they became one soul in two bodies. Her laughter was his happiness; while her sadness was his deepest sorrow. He hated to know that she was hurt or unhappy or sad. He would go to any extent, doing anything he could, just to bring her back to normal and to make her smile again.

They used to fight, but he made sure that the fight didn't last for so long. There were ups and downs in their relationship, yet it was beautiful. They were two different people, who were strangers once. But they fell in love in a way that felt eternal. It felt like the autumn in their life just turned to a beautiful spring.

He smiled whenever he heard her name. Her presence made him feel complete. She always had his shoulder to cry on, a place to rest and someone to vent to. They were each other's cheerleaders.

Love isn't always perfect, but it's beautiful.

Love isn't easy, it's quite difficult. In fact, it is, but even then, it's worth it. You protect each other, no matter how hurt you are. You laugh to see them smile, no matter how broken you are. When you are in love, all you think is about your partner. Just them….

All his thoughts were of her—NITARA…

and

Love.

More than a four letter word, which is easy to spell, but hard to define and impossible to live without.

But, she held something deep inside her heart. He didn't know what it was. She neither shared it with him nor did he ask her about it. But, he knew that it bothered her so much. It made her sad, so he never asked her about it and respected her privacy.

Chapter 3

The Fire

Days passed.

She is still in ICU. He was with her always after that. The burn marks were so clear on her face. She still has the oxygen mask on her face. The doctor said she is still in critical stage as her head hit so hard. But, he never lost hope because all he had was her. She was his whole world.

"You go home, take a shower, rest for a little time, and come back." Eka said, "I will stay with her till that!"

He nodded and went to the parking lot, got this car and drove home.

When he entered the house, it was silence. SILENCE.

That silence scared him. It didn't give peace, it haunted him in fact.

He went to their room. Their pictures were hung on the wall. That pictures hit him so hard. He sat on the bed and cried aloud. Those tears wouldn't stop, flowing like a waterfall. After so much time, he went to take a bath. When he came back, he went to the kitchen. He could still smell the fire. He didn't see it but he could feel it.

He was at his office and that's when Eka called him and said that Nitara had caught fire and she was taking her to the hospital. She also said that Nitara had fallen so hard that her head was bleeding.

That morning, Nitara told him that Eka was coming over to see her. She was busy preparing food for her. Eka later told him that when she entered the house, she saw Nitara lying on the floor, bleeding, with fire spreading through her dress.

He rushed to the hospital and saw her in the ICU. He felt like half of his heart had just been ripped out. When things around you hurt, you become quiet. That's what was happening with him. The whole surrounding hurted him in her absence, so he became silent. He fell asleep on the couch holding their wedding picture tightly to his heart.

How can someone be this special to a person that they would risk their whole life for them. Life is actually a miracle We never know what will happen next, and that's so scary because it hurts like hell.

Chapter 4

The Diary

It's 10 at night and its dark outside. He just woke up. The first thing he saw was their wedding photos that was hugged tight to his heart. Memories of your love hits hard when that person is not with you.

He went to the room and kept those pictures inside her shelf. That's where it was always kept. She keeps all her important and her most wanted thing there, inside her shelf. It was a mini version of her, filled with all her valuable treasures.

He kept the photos inside the shelf and took one of her clothes. All her clothes carried her smell. She smelled different—like pure, eternal love. LOVE.

His gaze falls on her dairy. He takes the dairy. The edges of that dairy was burned. He never read it before. He reconsiders before opening it.

Finally, he made the decision to read it.

He had seen that half-burned dairy before, but he felt like it wasn't the right time to read it. Now, he sensed that this was the moment for it.

SO HE PROCEEDED….

He went back to the couch, sat there comfortably and opened the dairy to start reading.

DAIRY

This dairy is about us - My first and only Love, NINAD...

From the day we met to....

-With Love
Nitara

July 26th 2016 is a date that I'll never forget. If that date had never existed, things would have been very different now. It was on July 26th,2015, that we saw each other for the first time. It was our fresher's day.

You know that moment when you see your soulmate for the first time? Your heart beats so fast, that you can feel it pounding, your cheeks become red and you hear your heart whispers "THAT'S YOUR SOULMATE!". I felt the same way. And I am sure that he felt it too because it was written in his eyes.

IT WAS LOVE AT FIRST SIGHT.

I still know how fast my heart beated that day. He wore a white shirt with light blue denim and he looked straight to my eyes. That gaze made me feel like something had pierced right through the center of my heart. I can never forget that look.

For the first time, I realized how special a pair of eyes can be. It's true that eyes have a language of their own; they spoke of the love that filled us.

PURE LOVE.

I still don't know how to explain that day in words. Some feelings are difficult to explain.

Chapter 5

Who Is He?

He closed the book. He wants to keep reading but something was stopping him. He wasn't feeling angry, he felt sad. Millions of thoughts raced through his mind.

WHO IS HE ACTUALLY?

WHY DID SHE BURN THE DAIRY?

WHAT HAPPENED IN BETWEEN?

WHY DIDN'T NITARA TELL ABOUT HIM?

And so on….

All he knew was the answers to his questions would surely be there in the book. So he decided to continue reading it.

Before starting to read he called Eka to make sure that everything is alright at the hospital. Eka told him that she would stay there with her tonight.

He ended the call and continued reading…

DAIRY

It's been almost two weeks since fresher's day and we both are in the same class, yet we haven't spoken to each other till now. I don't know why but I am still processing the day I first saw him. And I think that's the probable reason we both haven't talked till now. That picture of him is stuck in my head, living there rent-free.

I miss home. I miss seeing my mom and dad every day. The only relief I have now are the video calls we share. But still ... I miss them.

I don't know what this feeling is called, but a part of me still whispers that "HE IS MY SOULMATE". I want to talk to him. I want to tell him that I love him, but I don't know how to start.

The next day as usual I went to college but that morning, on my way to class, he sat just in front of me on the bus.

For the first few moments, I couldn't breathe. He sat just few seats in front of me and I guess he knew that my eyes were just glued to him. It's said that the faith of the mountain is to make way for the running water and the fate of my heart was to admire the eyes of this guy. In that moment I felt like I was ready to travel to the ends of the earth and far into the infinity if I have this beauty travelling with me. I knew I wouldn't stop adoring him because the way he smiles, he talks, he looks, his eyes and he himself deserves it. I couldn't see his face but for me his presence is more that, so I didn't care if all I could see was his back sticked to the chair. His voice made me fall for him even more. He turned back and I felt like his eyes were piercing right into the center my heart again and all I could see was him. Everything else surrounding me just vanished away.

"Ninad…!" someone called out again and his eyes shifted to the person sitting in the back of the bus.

NINAD…

Whenever we love a song or a tune, we play it on loop. That's the same thing I am doing now, but here the only difference is that it's a name.

And of course after hearing a song on repeat you might get bored, but the more I chanted his name, the more I fell for him. He looked back at me again. AGAIN... and smiled. Oh God!.... He smiled at me. I wished I could pause that moment. He smiled at me! I couldn't believe my eyes. His smile was eternal, something that could make you smile. And I smiled back.

We reached college and he got out of the bus before me. I exited after him and just for a moment, I was taken aback by what unfolded before me. He was there, anticipating my arrival by the bus. I was incredulous as I approached him; he greeted me with a smile, followed by the simple but significant word, "HI"

God…It was a dream come true moment. His voice sounded soo nice when i heard it up close. I stood frozen for a moment before finally replying him back, "Hi!".

We walk together to the classroom; we haven't talked anything till now except that HI. But I loved walking with him. It feels so nice. We reached the classroom, and stood there, waiting for one of us to talk. But neither of us did. We just stare at each other. God, his eyes. It was magical.

"Nitara" Eka called me.

God, why is she calling me now? He pointed his hands in her direction, telling me that I had to go. I didn't want to leave. I wanted to stay with him.

Mindlessly I walked over to her and sat next to her. He went to sit with his friend. He sat in backbench while I sat somewhere in middle.

"What's happening between you both?" She asked.

"Nothing!" I replied.

She knew that it was a lie, still she admitted it. Sir entered the class, took attendance and started teaching.

Here goes another day, the same as the other days, but today was quite different. I will never forget this day.

Chapter 6

Silence

He woke up the next morning having fallen asleep the last night. He checked his phone and found no calls missed. He freshed up, got ready and headed to the hospital.

It's just Ninad who is running in his mind now.

WHO IS HE? AND WHY IS NITARA TALKING SO MUCH ABOUT HIM?

Ninad, Ninad, Ninad …. That's all he could think about then.

He reaches the hospital, goes straight to the ICU. He go visits her. He wanted to ask her a millions of questions about Ninad but he stepped out of ICU and told Eka to go home now rest "I'll be here today," he assured her.

He then goes to the doctor's room and asked, "How is Nitara now? Can we shift her to room?".

"No!" the doctor said "she is still in a dangerous

stage. We need to monitor her, Abhi ".

Without replying a word back, he exited the room and sat in front of the ICU. Millions and Millions of thoughts raced through his mind. But there were no answers for any of them.

Silence surrounded him.

Then he remembered about the diary. He thought that the dairy might have answers to at least some of his questions. He took the dairy out of his bag and began to read it.

DAIRY

That day will always be pinned in the chapters of my life.

We talked to each other every day since that day. He waited for me outside the bus every morning so that we could go to class together. And every evening after class he waited for me so that we could leave together and catch the bus.

We never sat together on the bus or in class. He sat with his friends on the bus while I sat alone. In class, I sat with Eka, and he was with his friends. That evening, while returning back to the hostel, I sat on the bus alone, as usual and he sat with his friends. I was reading a book, when someone suddenly came and sat next to me.

It was him. I didn't need to glance to my side to confirm that it's him. I knew it was him. I knew what he smelled like. He smelled like those fresh flowers that had just bloomed. It wasn't those usual flowers; it was different.

I could smell his scent when he came and sat near me. He wrapped his arm around my shoulder and looked at me. Every time he looked at me, it felt like something was being pierced right in the center of my heart. I looked at him and there we were, sharing another eye-to–eye moment. It was clear in his eyes that he was falling for me, that he loved me.

"I am falling in love with you, Nitara" he told me and kissed my forehead.

I froze because I didn't expect that from him at that moment. I wanted to talk but my voice was not coming out of my throat. I wanted to tell him that I had fallen for him the first day we saw each other, but my voice wasn't coming out. I felt like I would stammer if I try to talk, but still I managed to tell him that,

"I fell in love with you since the day we first met..."

His eyes widened, he took his hands off from me, and hugged me. I closed my eyes tightly feeling our hearts finally coming together. All I could sense was our souls embracing each other.

I wished I could pause this moment. I wished we could hug together like this forever.

He didn't speak a word after that, he looked straight to my eyes and kissed my forehead and got off the bus as we reached the hostel.

Chapter 7

Deep Hugs

She was his first love but he wasn't her first love-Ninad was. It was a truth that he didn't want to accept. He wasn't jealous or angry, he was broken.

WHY DIDN'T NITARA TELL ANYTHING ABOUT HIM TO ME?

WHAT HAPPENED IN BETWEEN THEM?.. So many questions filled his mind.

"Abhi!", Nitara's mom called him. He stood up, holding the book behind him.

"Can we go see her now?" her mom asked. He nodded and watched her mom and dad getting into the ICU with their eyes filled with tears.

"how will they bear seeing her like this? After all, they are her birth givers. Why does God do this to good people?

His mind was filled with so many thoughts, yet he couldn't utter a single word. It felt like there were no words enough to describe his current state. Pain hugged him so tightly that he felt stuck, lost in it.

Darkness filled all over him. There was no sign of light anywhere.

Her parents came out of the ICU even more broken. Her father came to me and hugged me. He cried, and that hug made me cry too. You know that moment when you have to beg yourself to stop crying? He was going through that situation. He begged to her father to stop crying but those tears just didn't stop.

Her mom told Abhi, that they were going to stay there tonight with her. He nodded and watched them head down the lift to get their bags.

"how are they bearing this? Why is God making them suffer like this?" he thought. He sat down back in his seat and continued reading.

DAIRY

Every moment I spent with him felt so special. I think that's how you feel when you are in love. You wake up thinking about that person, you end your day thinking about them and you live your day thinking about them. That's love. Suddenly it felt like all love songs ever written, were just for us.

Yes, we are in love. We never said that to each other but we knew it: "We are in love". He has never left my mind since the first time we met. HE IS MINE AND I AM JUST HIS.

Our company was enough for us. Bad days turned good ones when I talked to him about it. And yes, I fell in love with a boy who loves my soul, a boy who brings light to my darkness, a boy who makes my life feel like heaven, a boy who makes me happy and I FELL IN LOVE WITH A BOY WHO IS SCARED OF LOSING ME.

He was exactly, precisely and perfectly what

I had been waiting for. I fall for him every day. My heart still skips a beat when he calls my name. My heart skips even more when he calls me MINE.

We met every day. He made me smile every day. He was my daily routine. A day without seeing him felt like hell. I still remember the day when he went to his home for three days because his grandmother was not well. I could neither message him nor call him as there was no signal there. Those three days felt like three decades. Those three DAYS were really hell.

When he returned after 3 days, I ran to the bus stop that morning and saw him getting of the bus. As soon as he stepped off the bus completely, I ran to him and hugged him so tight because I missed him so much. We always had so much to talk about and we never felt our company boring.

He could notice every change in my action whenever I was sad. He made sure that I always smiled and he never failed to make me laugh. Falling in love with him was the best thing that ever happened in my life. Everything seemed better when I was with him

Before I met him, I thought no one would love me and that I wouldn't fall in love with anyone. I believed nobody would be able to fill the void in my heart. But everything changed when I met him. He broke down all the barriers, opened my heart and walked straight through the center of it. He touched my soul and made me feel complete. He made me feel alive. Now I realize that I AM HOPELESSLY IN LOVE WITH YOU, NINAD.

Chapter 8

HIM

With a heavy heart, he closed the book. " But What's so SPECIAL about HIM? "he muttered. Each page made him wonder about what happened in between them.

He missed her so much. Every time he thought of her, he realized how much she meant to his life. He missed her so much and he knew that pain was worth it because SHE IS GOING TO COME BACK. His world was just her and he hadn't allowed anyone else to enter that world because she was enough for him. She is the reason he was living for.

SHE..

NITARA..

The pain of the waiting was unbearable but if that waiting means getting to spend the rest of his life with her, then he was ready for it.

Its true LOVE IS HEAVEN BUT IT HURTS

LIKE HELL. People say love is supposed to Heal You, but that's not entirely true. Love can heal some things, but not everything. However, when it hurts, it never hurts a part of you, it hurts you completely.

Have you ever felt the pain of losing someone with whom you planned your entire life and future? It hurts, it hurts like hell.

He sat there in front of the ICU. NUMB Not knowing what to do. His world was fighting for life inside that room, and he couldn't do a single thing to help her. If he could have, he would have already given his entire life to her., but the truth was he couldn't. That's it: "LOVE HURTS LIKE HELL, IT NEVER HEALS YOU!"

Chapter 9

Memories

He spent that whole day in the hospital with her. The next morning, he returned to meet the doctor and asked if she could be shifted to a room. The doctor replied with a "NO again." He told Abhi that she is in the same stage since day one. DANGEROUS."

He exited the room and saw Eka coming.

"Hi" Abhi said, forcing a smile.

"Hey how is she now?" Eka asked

"No change" he said with tears filled in his eyes.

"Be strong Abhi, she will be alright." Eka assured him.

He nods his head, wishing for her to come back. He went straight to the washroom, and stared right into the mirror. Dark bags hung under his eyes. Sleep becomes so hard when you can't stop thinking. Every piece of him ached for her.

His mind currently felt like the hardest puzzle to

solve. He had billions and billions of questions racing through his mind but there was no answer for any of them. Those questions were stuck in his head, living there rent free.

Happy memories hurt you the most when you are trying not to think about them. Those joyful moments they spent together played right in front of him in the mirror. Those butterflies he used to feel in his stomach whenever he saw her or heard her voice are dead now. He felt heartless, Emotionless, Alone.. Lonely..

He cried so hard until there were no tears left. He washed his face and stepped out of the washroom. His eyes were red and his face looked swollen. This was the darkest time of his life.

Today, his forest felt dark. There is no sense of light. All the tress was sad and the butterflies that once danced around are dead now. He thought about how deeply he had fallen for her, that every single second without her felt like hell. He felt dead deep inside his heart.

DEAD.

Chapter 10

A Battle With Life

He saw Eka coming out of the ICU, and they both sat down in the chairs nearby the ICU.

"Are you okay?" Eka asked him.

Those words again broke him into tears.

"I don't know, but I feel like a part of me is dead now." Abhi replied.

"Don't lose your hope, Abhi.. She will come back. Everything is hard before it gets easy." Eka told him.

"Why is this happening to me, Eka?" He asked.

She remained silent and that silence felt like the answer.

"Trust me Abhi, if she belongs to you, she will come back just for you." Eka said softly.

Silence surrounded them again. The quieter you become, the more you can hear your inner voice. He could hear everything his inner voice was telling him.

The Emergency alarm blared from the ICU. Abhi jumped to his feet and rushed into the room. She was fighting for her life. Doctors and nurses rushed into the ICU. He stood there helpless, watching her fight for her life.

He was praying to god so desperately.

What else could he do now?

Chapter 11

Dyingful

It's been almost 45 minutes now. Abhi had been waiting outside the ICU. Tears were flowing down his cheeks. Eka was also there with him. They Both were soaked in tears. When the doctor finally came out, Abhi rushed to him and asked, "How is she? Is she okay?"

"I don't know, Abhi. If you ask me if she is okay now, she isn't. She is in a lot of pain. Her right side is getting paralyzed, Abhi. Her brain ..it's.." the doctor paused, struggling to find the right words, the seriousness of the situation is clear in his eyes.

He stood there numb, not able to process what the doctor had just said

He stared at her through the glass door of the ICU, fully aware of the pain she was enduring. He sat down and closed his eyes, trying to come to terms with what the doctor had just said.

Pain.

Silence.

That's what he could breathe in then.

Chapter 12

Memories Never Die

It had been now 2 weeks and 3 days now. He had gone home just once during this time, staying with her the whole time. She remained in critical condition, her right side completely paralyzed and her left side also showing signs of paralysis.

He held on to hope that she would come back because all he had was her. His heart felt so heavy, and he couldn't express the thoughts in his head. He had many questions, but none had answers.

Silence consumed him. Pain lived inside him, and the fear of losing her broke him down. Words were stuck in his throat, fighting to come out, but nothing came out. A haunting silence surrounded him.

Memories never die. All the moment they spent together, both good and bad, replayed constantly in his mind. He missed her deeply and he was certain that she missed him too.

Chapter 13

Reality

Next morning Eka saw Abhi sitting there in front of the ICU. He hadn't eaten anything and hadn't slept. He looked exhausted, but he refused to leave her side. The thought of leaving her alone filled him with fear.

Eka came and sat beside him. "Go home, Abhi. You need some rest. I'll stay with her today. Come by tomorrow morning," she said gently.

"No, Eka. I want to stay with her. I'm scared to leave her alone," he replied, his voice trembling.

"There's no need to be scared, Abhi. I'll stay with her. I won't leave her alone," she reassured him.

He reluctantly accepted her offer, trusting Eka since she was Nitara's best friend. They were best since childhood, going to the same school, college, and even working together. He entered the ICU, glanced at her, then made his way to the parking lot and headed home. Eka also told him to take some clothes for Nitara.

Once he reached home, he went straight to their bedroom. He took a shower, ate lunch, and continued reading the diary.

DAIRY

Time flew by so fast. Days had become so much nicer since he entered my life, filled with more color and joy. I enjoyed being with him and I knew he did too. I am not saying that we never had fights, we had our fights, but we made sure they didn't last long. We made sure that, at the end of the day we talked to each other and wrapped things up on a good note.

Our days began and ended with our calls. He was not a chapter of my life, he was the whole book of my life. His eyes turned everything into a poetry. A poem, only I could read, meant only for me because those eyes were mine and that man was mine.

I could see my future when I looked in his eyes. His eyes were something magical, PURE, ETERNAL...

I didn't want to lose him, and neither did he. We could never imagine a life without each other. We were two bodies but one soul. He was my whole world, my entire universe. Above all, HE MADE MY EXISTENCE BEAUTIFUL.

Words cannot express the butterflies in my stomach whenever I thought about him or saw him.

He is my everything.
A day without him felt like hell.

Chapter 14

Her Story

Someone rang the doorbell. He closed the diary and stood up to go open the door. As he did, some papers slipped from the diary and fell onto the bed. He picked them up to see what they were, but the doorbell rang again, so he rushed to the door and opened it. It was the food he had ordered. He took the bags and set them on the table. Then he went to the couch, sat there and opened those papers.

It was a letter written by Nitara.

"Dear Abhi, " that's how the letter started.

"A letter for me?" he muttered in curiosity.

He decided to read it.

LETTER

Dear Abhi,

I am writing this letter in the hope that one day you will read it. There is something I've wanted to tell you one thing since the day we met. But I was not mentally prepared to tell that to you aloud, so I thought it would be better to write it down. Please read the whole letter, Abhi, and don't be angry with me afterward. Don't hate me, either.

I love you so much, Abhi. You were the light in my darkness. To say that I love you so much would be the most understatement of my life. You make me sublimely happy.

It feels like yesterday, when I think about the day we met for the first time. You know that I was not in the right state of mind at that time. But you never asked me what the matter was. Instead you cared for me, you made sure that I was safe and happy.

It was NINAD who bothered me. It was him who constantly troubled me. But you never asked about my past. You made sure that my present and future would be the best.

You soothe and inspire me, encouraging me to look out for solutions when I can't find any. You taught me that PAIN isn't constant, it heals but a part of that pain will always remain. You made sure that I wasn't in pain and my pain affected you more than it affected me.

Nothing is more beautiful than waking up next to you.

You helped me to restore my faith in love and in people. You taught me to fall in love again, and I chose to fall in love with you. There is one thing I want to tell you is about NINAD. He was my first and only love before I met you. He was my everything. I woke up every morning thinking that I could see him.

But, the world wasn't ready for us. Destiny had other plans forus.

Everyone told me to move on, "MOVE ON, NITARA"
It's just SIX LETTERS,

And TWO WORDS.
It's EASY TO SAY,
But HARD TO EXPLAIN
And HARDER TO DO.
MOVE ON!

No one understood how I felt, but you did. You were the only one who truly got me. And the funniest part is that you never asked me what was bothering me. Abhi, there's a diary in my shelf. Just take it and read it. You will understand everything. But please don't hate me. I can't bear another heartbreak.

Do you remember that day when I went for my college get-together? Everyone over there was talking about Ninad, and me, I was just trying to get out of the scariest truth of my life, NINAD. Hearing everyone, talk about him triggered my emotions. I ran out of that gathering in the middle and rushed to my apartment. I was shivering, my heart was racing, and I was sweating too hard.

You called me several times, but I couldn't pick up. My phone was silent that day. I ran to my apartment, went straight to the shower and opened the tap and stood there for almost half an hour. That's when you rushed over to my apartment room. I still remember that day so clearly.

You ran to my room, searching for me, and found me sitting there down in the cold shower. I was shivering so hard that I couldn't talk, and I was crying so much that I couldn't breathe. You rushed to the bathroom and turned off the shower, then grabbed a towel and rubbed my head. You were shouting at me for sitting there in the cold shower.

You helped me out of the shower and told me to change my clothes. By the time I changed my clothes and came to the living room, you prepared hot coffee for us. When you saw me shivering, you came near me and hugged me tight. AND THAT'S WHEN I FELL FOR YOU, ABHI. That's when I realized that you were the one my heart had been longing for.

We shared that coffee together on my couch, and all I remember after that is waking up the next morning in the couch with blankets around me and a letter on the table that read,

"Good Moring, Nitara. You fell asleep on the

couch last night, so I covered you with a blan-
ket and left. Hope you have a good day Nitara.

-With love,
Abhi.''

That smile I had while reading that note that day has never vanished from my face till now. Then you proposed me and I didn't even have to think twice to say YES.

I love you Abhi. I love you to the moon and back.

And Ninad, I loved him and he loved me back too but…. destiny had planned something else for us.

Destiny planned something brighter for me, and I am grateful for that to God.

I started living my life to its fullest when you entered to it. I truly want to spend the rest of my life with you. If it hadn't been for you, I would have never made it till here Abhi. I love you soo much. Please read the letter and don't hate me.

-With lots of love,
Your Nitara.

Chapter 15

Lost

He placed the letter down with tears soaking his face. He never knew she loved him this much. It's true, distance shows you the value of a person.

He wanted to rush to her and hug her tight, but....

He took the car keys and drove to the hospital. He needed to tell her how much he loved her and how much that letter meant to him.

As he drove, his phone rang. It was Eka calling. He answered the call.

"Hello!" Abhi said.

"Come to the hospital fast" Eka replied. She was panicked and scared.

He drove even more faster to the hospital. when he reached there, he saw Eka crying hard. There were several nurses inside the ICU, and the doctor was just coming out. He rushed over to the doctor and asked, "What's wrong doctor?"

"Her whole body is paralyzed now Abhi, and

her brain is declining too. She is in so much pain" the doctor paused for a moment and continued,

"It's better we let her go, Abhi..."

"No!" he exclaimed

"No doctor, no... I can't bear that. I am ready to do anything for her but not this." he burst into tears.

"There's nothing left to do Abhi. She doesn't have much time left. I am sorry, but it's better to let her go soon because she is suffering, "the doctor said gently.

"No," he muttered, his heart breaking.

"Think about her Abhi, consider the pain she is suffering and then decide what you want and tell me." the doctor said before leaving.

He felt like he is dead. It's just his body with no soul because his soul and everything was Nitara.

He entered the ICU and sat beside her, holding her hand as his tears fell onto her skin. "Please don't leave me, Nitara," he begged.

Her heart rate spiked on the monitor.

"I know you are hearing me Nitara. Please don't leave me and go. I want to spend my whole life with you. I love you so much, and I don't know how to express that in words. I read your letter

Nitara. I can never hate you."

Tears streamed down his face.

"You have no idea how much I love you and how much that letter means to me. I fell for you since the day we first met and my love for you is increasing day by day. Please don't leave me, Nitara. PLEASE..."

Chapter 16

The Untold Truth

He stepped out of the ICU and sat down in the chair in front of it.

Praying was all he could do then.

Suddenly he remembered about Ninad.

What happened to him? Nitara told to read the diary but it was at home.

He rushed back, grabbed the diary and the letter, and hurried back to the hospital.

Sitting down in front of the ICU, he opened the diary and began to read.

DIARY

It was just hours left for 26th July 2016. We were going to celebrate our first anniversary together. I had a special plan in mind: I was going to propose to him.

11: 56

11: 57

11: 58

11:59

12: 00, July 26 2016.

Midnight arrived, marking July 26th, 2016. I called him, asking him to come to my hostel, but he didn't answer. I kept calling—three times, four times, six times, ten times—but he still wasn't picking up.

I felt tense, though I didn't know why. There was a bad feeling deep down in my heart. I decided to call one of his friends, but he wasn't answering either. I tried calling him again.

15 times.

20 times. Still no response.

I stood outside my hostel, waiting, until almost 2:45 in the night. Then Eka told me to go inside and try to sleep. I went to bed, but I couldn't sleep. That bad feeling in my heart just wouldn't go away. I ignored it and kept on calling him. I felt like time was dragging that night, it felt like it stretched into 2 decades. I called him around 150 times until morning.

When I woke up morning, I got ready and went to college. He wasn't there on the bus and none of his friends were either. I could sense that sinking feeling deep down there but I ignore it and kept calling him.

When I reached at the college, I noticed a huge crowd near the notice board. Anxiously I rushed over to see what was stuck there, that had drawn the attention of the whole campus.

I pushed through the crowd and read the notice.

"HEARTFELT CONDOLONCES TO NINAD." it said.

I couldn't believe my eyes. I read it again, hoping I was mistaken.

But no, the words were clear: "HEARTFELT CONDOLENCES TO NINAD."

He had left this world that day.

He had left me alone.

I struggled to push my way out of the crowd, I broke down into tears. I have never cried like that before in my entire life.

He died? My mind couldn't grasp it.

Someone touched my shoulders, I turned back to see who it is. It was one his friends.

"Ninad…." He began, his voice was heavy.

"He left the hostel last night by 11:00 pm. He wanted to surprise you and propose since today was your first anniversary together. He took my bike and headed out. But on the way, the bike collided with a car. The car didn't even stop to check on him. We reviewed the CCTV footage. Around midnight, I got a call from his number. I answered it and a stranger told me that Ninad got hit by a car and was in the hospital. By the time I reached there. He left this world. I saw all your missed calls today morning. He paused for a moment, and continued,

A random person found him lying in the road covered in blood, and took him to the hospital, but it was too late." he says.

Then he handed me a gift box and a letter.

"This was the gift he had with him for you. That man who found him gave this to me." he said quietly.

"Open it when you feel it's the right time." he told before leaving.

I collapsed and cried harder than I ever had that day.

The next day, I found the courage to open the box. Inside, there was a ring. I burst into tears again.

I opened the letter and it said,

Dear Nitara,

I have been waiting for this day to make you completely mine. I have already given a major part of my heart to you but today, from now on it's completely yours. I am just yours Nitara..., and you are just mine. Today is the day I am going you propose you. I'm not sure how to do it, but I am going to do this. You are the sunshine to my darkness. I can't think about a single moment living without you. I may forget myself, but I'll never forget you."

"I want to hold your hand and walk down those quiet, empty roads, listening to music

together. I want to take rest lying on your shoulders and more than anything I WANT TO LIVE THE REST OF MY LIFE WITH YOU, NITARA. I love you more day by day and I feel incomplete when you are not around. A day without talking to you feels like hell. "Meeting you was like listening to a story and knowing it would be my all-time, forever favorite.

I belong to you; - every inch of me and every part of my flesh, every beat of my heart and every breathe I take is yours.

My heart is yours; yours to love, yours to hold, yours to hug and yours to kiss. But please don't break it.

Promise me you are mine,
JUST MINE.
I LOVE YOU SO MUCH NITARA.
YOU'RE MINE.

I put the letter down and cried my eyes out.

At that moment, I understood that "FOREVER DOSEN'T MEAN FOREVER".

Maybe in another universe, we will be together.

Maybe someday, in some way, in a universe far away, I will meet him and we will never be apart.

Chapter 17

THEM

He turned the pages after, but that was it. Nothing more.

"Why is God being so cruel to good people?". He thought.

He then rushed to Eka and asked,

"Who is NINAD?"

"Did you read her dairy?" she replied him back, concern showing on her face.

"Yes" he responded handling her the dairy and the letter. His eyes were filled with tears, and his cheeks were soaked with them.

"It wasn't easy for her, Abhi. She went through a very lot after that. She even tried to take her own life once, and that's when I took her to a therapist. She was in depression for three years. Her therapist suggested her to write about him in a dairy and then burn that book, but she never did that. She wrote it down and kept it with her instead. Therapy was not helping her, but then she met you. You were the light in her darkness, the life in her world. She started recovering after you came into her life. You mean everything to her, Abhi. EVERYTHING." she replied.

He hugged Eka and cried aloud. He felt lost and that she had loved him more than anything— THE MOST.

Chapter 18
The Worst Pain

He entered the ICU and sat by her side for what felt like an eternity. Finally, he kissed her forehead and stepped out to speak with the doctor. He asked the doctor to free her from this pain and signed all the necessary documents The doctor went inside the ICU and returned after some time. Abhi stayed outside, unable to bear watching her vanish away.

When the doctor came out, he said softly, "She's free from pain now, Abhi. I know the Lord is with her. Let her soul go to heaven. I'm so sorry for your loss."

He entered the ICU, feeling broken, and burst into tears.

Sitting by her side, he whispered, "I'm sorry," but he couldn't complete the whole sentence as he was crying that hard.

He made this choice because he didn't want her to suffer any longer. She had endured so much pain for so long, and he couldn't bear the thought of her suffering anymore. So, he set her free from all the suffering in her life.

And, it was a JULY 26th.

Chapter 19

A Dead Soul

A part of him died that day, because his heart belonged to her. ONLY HER.

Chapter 20

Time Heals Nothing

He stood there in the dark night, on the top of the hospital building, not knowing what to do. He felt that he had lost something that meant everything to him. He wanted to cry aloud but something was stopping him. He wanted to scream at the sky and ask God why he did this? But something held him back. He felt utterly alone. He felt as if his entire life had shattered into pieces. He couldn't put back those pieces together. He kept on thinking of it that night. Tears fell from his eyes; he stood there, frozen, lost in his grief.

He blamed himself for not staying home that day. He kept thinking that if he had been there, none of this would have happened. That night felt soo long. He didn't know how he would survive after that night. He didn't actually know how he would survive his whole life in the absence of his love. He felt empty. He felt alone. He felt that his whole life was a lie. He felt like his past was a dream that he could never forget. He wanted that time back, but the truth is that he couln't get that back. He was not ready to accept the truth. But he had no other way. He had to accept the truth, but the past and his memories was not allowing him to do that. He had no other way than to accept the truth.

He said, "Time heals nothing!" Tears streamed down his face as he spoke those words.

In fact, its true. Time heals nothing. It only leaves a scar which will never fade. Time changes people but it never heals memories. It teaches us how to leave with that pain. Some memories haunt you for a lifetime, yet those memories will be the best of what you have.

At that moment he understood, "PEOPLE

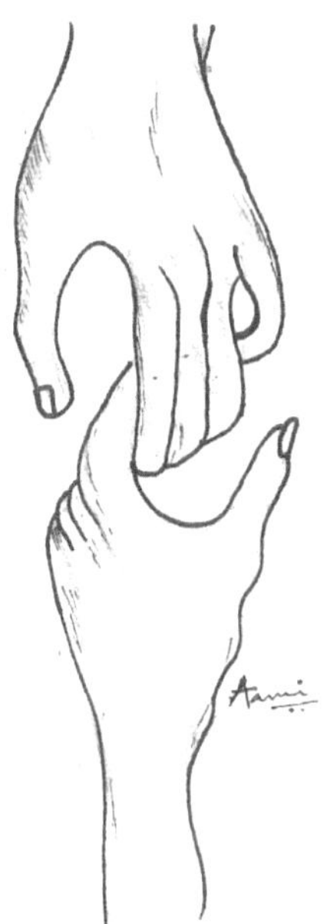

LEAVE NOT MEMORIES". Some truths are very hard to digest but you have to accept it completely. He felt as if the whole city was silent that night. The moon was absent and he believed that the moon was crying behind the clouds for his loss. Nothing can compensate for what he had lost – NOTHING.

He closed his eyes tightly and said, "Sometime the distance you have with someone destroys you completely, but it teaches you the value of that person".